WOLVES

NORTH AMERICAN ANIMAL DISCOVERY LIBRARY

Lynn M. Stone

Rourke Corporation, Inc.
Vero Beach, Florida 32964

PHOTO CREDITS

All photos by author

LIBRARY OF CONGRESS
Library of Congress Cataloging-in-Publication Data
Stone, Lynn M., 1942-
  Wolves / by Lynn M. Stone.

    p. cm. — (North American animal discovery library)
    Summary: An introduction to the physical characteristics,
habits, and natural environment, and future prospects of the
North American wolf.
    ISBN 0-86593-044-9
    1. Wolves—Juvenile literature. [1. Wolves.] I. Title.
II. Series: Stone, Lynn M., 1942- North American animal
discovery library.
QL737.C22S77   1990
599.74'442—dc20   89-70169
                              CIP
                              AC

TABLE OF CONTENTS

THE WOLF

In many children's stories, wolves *(Canis lupus)* are big and bad. Wolves certainly are big. But wolves (also known as timber or gray wolves) aren't bad.

Wolves are **predators,** which means that they hunt and kill other animals for food. Wild wolves, however, are rarely, if ever, a threat to people.

Wolves live together in organized family groups called **packs.** Members of a pack work together and make good parents.

Wolves are well known for their long, loud howls.

Wolf

THE WOLF'S COUSINS

The gray wolf's cousins are in the dog family. The wolf's closest relative is the red wolf *(Canis rufus)*. The red wolf is an altogether different animal than the gray wolf, which is the subject of this book.

Red wolves look much like gray wolves, but they are much smaller. Red wolves are larger than foxes and coyotes, which are also wild dogs.

Red wolves used to live in the southeastern United States. They are now nearly **extinct.**

Arctic Fox

HOW THEY LOOK

An adult wolf could be mistaken for a German Shepherd dog. A wolf, however, has a larger, wider head than a dog.

A wolf may weigh up to 175 pounds, and wolves often weigh over 100 pounds. A male wolf may stand over 42 inches tall at its shoulder and be six and one-half feet long.

Wolves are usually gray, but they may be black, brown, white, or a combination of colors. Their long, dense fur keeps them warm, and they have long, bushy tails.

White Wolf

WHERE THEY LIVE

Wolves used to live throughout most of North America. They lived in forests, on prairies, and on the **tundra** of the Far North.

Today the **range,** or living area, of wolves is much smaller than it was 150 years ago. Most North American wolves live in the forests and on the tundra of Canada and Alaska.

A few hundred wolves live in northeastern Minnesota. A few more live in northwestern Montana, northern Wisconsin, and on Isle Royale National Park in Michigan.

Wolf in snow

Wolf at rest

Wolves eating deer

HOW THEY LIVE

Wolves hunt together. Adults in a pack find and kill **prey,** the animals that they hunt.

Wolf packs are made up of a wolf family or of several wolf families. Large packs have more than 30 wolves.

Wolves fight among themselves to decide leaders. Each pack has a male and female pair who lead.

Wolves usually hunt at night. They may walk several miles, then return to a home den the next morning.

A wolf den is usually a burrow in a hillside or in the ground

Wolf pack

THE WOLF'S PUPS

The pack's female leader is usually the only one in the pack to have pups. She will have from five to 14 pups in her **litter,** or group of babies.

They stay in the den for nearly a month. They first live on their mother's milk and on soft food. As they grow older, the wolves eat the adults' prey.

Wolf pups learn to hunt by following the pack. At two years of age, they are nearly adults.

Wolves live from 10 to 18 years.

Wolf pup

PREDATOR AND PREY

Whenever possible, wolves kill large animals, such as deer, moose, and caribou. If they cannot find or catch a large animal, wolves will gobble up mice, birds, fish, or beavers.

Wolves have keen eyesight, hearing, and smell. They are strong and fast, but they don't like to take chances. They usually don't attack big, healthy male animals, like bull moose. Instead, they are more likely to kill old, sick, or hurt animals.

In a long chase, many animals, such as deer, can outrun wolves.

Wolf eating prey

WOLVES AND PEOPLE

People have often thought of wolves as being a danger to themselves and to their animals. As far back as the 1600s, wolves were shot and trapped wherever they were found. Even the United States government once paid its agents to poison wolves.

Wild wolves almost never attack people. Yet people have made wolves an **endangered** animal, in danger of disappearing.

The good news for wolves is that many people now realize that wolves are not a danger. They view wolves as bright, handsome animals.

Wolf at rest

THE WOLF'S FUTURE

Wolves in Europe are nearly extinct - gone forever. Although endangered in many places, North American wolves have a brighter future than their European cousins.

Many people and groups have rushed to support the idea of saving, rather than shooting, wolves.

Wolves do well when they are protected. But the wolf's future also depends upon the protection of its home.

Wolves need huge areas of wild land. Protecting wild lands will help protect these great wild dogs.

Glossary

endangered (en DANE jerd)—in danger of no longer existing; very rare

extinct (ex TINKT)—no longer existing

litter (LIH ter)—a group of babies born together of the same mother

pack (PAK)—a family or families of wolves that live together

predator (PRED a tor)—an animal that kills other animals for food

prey (PRAY)—an animal that is hunted by another for food

range (RAYNJ)—the entire area in which a certain type of animal lives

tundra (TUN dra)—the cold, treeless land of the Far North

INDEX